BRINGING WORLDS

TOGETHER

BY LAINEY HITCHMAN

BRINGING WORLDS TOGETHER

Cross Cultural Marriage Series Book 1

Copyright © 2016 by Lainey Hitchman

Cover by: Lainey Hitchman
Editor: Roy Hitchman

ISBN: 9781911176022

Book Website
www.hitchedtogether.com
Email: info@hitchedtogether.com

Give feedback on the book at:
feedback@hitchedtogether.com

BRINGING WORLDS

†OGETHER

BY LAINEY HITCHMAN

BOOK 1

† CULTURAL MARRIAGE SERIES

OTHER BOOKS IN THIS SERIES

Acknowledgments

Writing this book not only has been a journey for me but those in my company. My family and friends have been my sounding boards and constant encouragers. I love and appreciate my weird and wonderful international family. Those who are truly cross-cultural will understand that in the term, 'family' I include many precious friends.

Preface

The world seems to be becoming a smaller and smaller place. Easier transport and the development of technologies such as video conferencing and dating websites means that cross-cultural marriages are on the increase. We knew that not only were the numbers of intercultural couples great, but their needs were great too. Our concern was that in writing a book about cross-cultural marriage not every single nuance of cultural difference could be addressed. There are too many cultures and too many combinations to set that as a realistic goal. Our conclusion was to write this book, a book which deals with general principles you can establish which, when applied, make a cross-cultural marriage strong, healthy and vibrant.

As you read, you will get to know us and our family and our friends a little better. Our hope is that our transparency about our failures and successes will speak to your hearts and that it will also make a difference in how you grow in your cross-cultural marriage.

CONTENTS

THE
IMPORTANCE
OF CULTURE

Culture is a Big Deal

Another day, another impasse. At least that is what it felt like for the newlyweds. Getting used to each other was one thing, but neither of them could have anticipated so many disagreements. They were especially concerned that the issues between them seemed so petty. Why had which way the toilet roll went on the toilet roll holder become such a big issue? Who really cared where to squeeze the toothpaste? So what if the toilet seat is left up or down! Yet, if these truly were unimportant issues why defend them so much? Why not just change and adapt? Therein lay the problem, both husband and wife wanted the other one to change. They were right, the other was wrong, that was the bottom line. What they didn't realise was that they were in a cross-cultural marriage and culture was playing havoc with their lives. They were wired from birth to disagree, and they desperately needed to learn how to get on the same page instead of fretting about the 'small stuff' and allowing pet peeves to come between them.

Perhaps you are wondering, 'aren't those typical marriage problems'? They are! It would be easy for me to begin with a story of a culture clash between European and Asian spouses or between an African husband and his North American wife but cultures intersect in many different ways. We often dismiss the 'small' issues and don't realise what we are dealing with is actually a culture clash. That's because we usually have preconceived ideas regarding what a cross-cultural marriage is. When some hear the term cross-cultural relationship, they imagine a couple who come from different continents, others will imagine a couple who each speak a different mother tongue, some will think of couples who have come from two different religious backgrounds and others will think of a couple from two different ethnic backgrounds. You will undoubtedly have your own idea of what defines a cross-cultural marriage. You may be surprised though to find that it is much more than you first thought! In fact, all relationships are to some degree cross-cultural simply because no two families are the same! While the word 'culture' can be applied to the broad brush stroke of a people-group, it can also apply to the microcosm of an individual family.

So why is culture such a big deal? A little research reveals that culture goes to the depths of what defines a person. It is so difficult to explain fully that many definitions have been offered. One definition I particularly like is from Texas A&M University. It outlines culture as the following: "Culture refers to the cumulative deposit of knowledge, experience, beliefs, values, attitudes, meanings, hierarchies, religion, notions of time, roles, spatial relations, concepts of the universe, and material objects and possessions acquired by a group of people in the course of generations through individual and group striving". Wow, that's a long list! In other words, culture infiltrates our interactions on almost every subject and approach to life. It's a 'big deal' because it is integral to how we live life and how we do relationships. Culture can't just be ignored!

In light of this definition, it is safe to say that culture, which permeates through so many aspects of our lives, will undoubtedly have an impact on marriage. You may not have realised that some of the issues you are facing are cultural. Step back and for a moment take a second look at the things you have been squabbling about. Why is it that you feel so strongly? If your answer is that it's a black and white issue, then you are probably dealing with culture. Why is it that you feel your spouse is wrong, and your way is the only way to do something? It is certainly possible that it all boils down to cultural differences. The greater the cross-cultural differences in a relationship, the greater the need for learning about each other's cultures and understanding each other's backgrounds. If you take the time to figure out why your spouse thinks the way they do it can transform your marriage.

Many years ago Roy and I stumbled across a truth which helped us a lot in our relationship. In the book of Proverbs, three words are often used interchangeably. We had always thought it was simply that the writer used the three words as synonyms however we were mistaken. Those three words were KNOWLEDGE, UNDERSTANDING and WISDOM and they don't mean the same thing at all! We realised that God was trying to get our attention and that we needed to understand what He was actually saying. You see, having knowledge was good; knowledge being the facts you have learned about something. Having 'understanding' is better; when you move towards understanding you are more able to discern the 'why' behind the behaviour.

I know, for example, that Roy does not like to wait for people. That's a fact; I know that about him. Finally, I took the time to dig a little deeper and see if there was a particular reason why. The answer surprised me. I discovered that when he was a child he used to spend a long time waiting for his grandfather. I could imagine him as a young boy waiting outside the pub where he had been instructed to stand while his grandfather downed some pints of beer with his friends. The time would almost stand still; waiting was not just uncomfortable, it was not a happy memory. That story of Roy's childhood helped me gain an understanding of why Roy was impatient while he was waiting for me, why he would come across as 'unduly' frustrated. Although this knowledge didn't 'fix' the issue, it certainly helped to have a better understanding of why he felt the way he did.

It is often difficult to know what to do with the information we have. Should you just take note of it and leave it at that? I believe that there is one further step which is important. While knowledge is a good thing to have and understanding is even better, wisdom is best. Wisdom is reached when you know what to do with the information with which you are armed. Wisdom enables you to act well on what you know and understand. Wisdom can bring harmony while understanding may only bring tolerance. For a long time, armed with the information that Roy didn't like to wait, I tolerated his impatience. If he was a bit grumpy when he was waiting for me, I gave him a bit of extra grace, but the problem didn't go away. Often when we are at a loss and don't know what to do in a situation, we simply pray. Roy's impatience while waiting, was one of those situations. We know that true wisdom comes from God, our designer. He knows how He created you, He understands why you behave the way you do, and He has the wisdom to help you make your cross-cultural marriage work.

In our case we both needed to change, I needed to be clear about the time something was going to take, and Roy needed to work on his attitude. I also needed to break some bad habits. Change is not easy, but it was definitely not impossible, we are living proof!

PROVERBS 2:6 ESV
FOR THE LORD GIVES WISDOM;
FROM HIS MOUTH COME KNOWLEDGE AND UNDERSTANDING;

- What are the signs that you are in a cross-cultural marriage?

- Are you willing to go on a journey to learn more about each other?

- In which areas do you already know that you need understanding and wisdom?

Our Cross-cultural Marriage

I remember the first time I saw Roy; he was exceptionally tall and skinny. My attention turned his way because of the strong English accent that rang out in a room crowded with people from Northern Ireland. He was distinctive and immediately captured my attention. I was introduced to him in the university canteen by a mutual friend affectionately known as 'Ronan the Barbarian' (I don't think Ronan was ever aware of this nickname). I'm amazed that I can still remember so many details of that day. I was drinking my tenth cup of coffee trying to get enough energy to do the English assignment that awaited me; Roy had just returned from a training session with QUB[1] rowing club. Roy was different from the other guys I knew. I liked that. I remember feeling attracted to him because he stood out from the crowd. That day marked the beginning of a friendship that later blossomed into a relationship, a relationship which demanded we make an effort to learn how to bridge the gaps between our differences. What attracted us to each other also caused us some issues in relating to each other.

You might feel that the differences between the Northern Irish and English cultures are not too mammoth. Admittedly we didn't have to learn a new language to

1   Queens University Belfast

16

communicate, nor cross the world to live together, however, we did meet many cultural challenges. It often seemed that we had been wired completely differently and in many respects that is true, but God has given us the ability to work through our cultural differences and enjoy a happy, healthy marriage.

As Roy and I have ministered to couples over the last few decades, we have been able to share some principles which helped us in our cross-cultural relationship. It became apparent that many couples were struggling with the type of issues we had encountered and were muddling through trying to find solutions. That caused us to think about why we should all muddle through, surely we could learn from one another! That thought was the beginning of a process which resulted in this book. We have drawn on the experience of others to discover some of the difficulties that greater cross-cultural contrasts bring to the table.

- Share what it was that attracted you to each other.

- Were there any elements of each other's cultures which you found off-putting?

Psalm 139:13-15 (Amp)

For You did form my inward parts;
You did knit me together in my mother's womb.
I will confess and praise You
for You are fearful and wonderful
and for the awful wonder of my birth!
Wonderful are Your works,
and that my inner self knows right well.
My frame was not hidden from You
when I was being formed in secret
[and] intricately and curiously wrought
[as if embroidered with various colours]
in the depths of the earth
[a region of darkness and mystery].

Your Unique Culture

Your Unique Culture

The first thing you need to recognise about your personal culture is that it is unique, just as you are unique. That might sound obvious, however, too often when we think of culture we do so purely in terms of the country of origin. Stereotypical behaviours pop into the mind, and many assumptions are made as a result.

The reality is that your culture is not just the product of your country of origin it has been formed in many multifaceted layers. Culture includes your language, your faith, your education, your life experiences and your family background. These elements blend together to form someone who is absolutely unique.

If your spouse read a book about your country or your culture, it would be fair to say that their background knowledge may have improved, but it would not mean that they know you. Don't fall into the trap of assumption. As you work through this book together, use it as an opportunity to get to know each other better. Talk about your past, your present and your expectations for the future. Go beyond the headlines and be willing to express the things that are a little more difficult to put into words. You will reap the rewards for the effort you invest in this process.

Your culture is also defined by your individual ethics

and belief system. These convictions cannot be easily dismissed because it includes principles which you hold dear. There are values which run deep to your core and play a part in every decision you make. Your personal culture is much like your fingerprints; they may have similarities to others, but they are exclusive to you.

"VALUES ARE LIKE FINGERPRINTS. NOBODY'S ARE THE SAME, BUT YOU LEAVE 'EM ALL OVER EVERYTHING YOU DO."
ELVIS PRESLEY

A question that is often used to help people get to know each other is, "If you had sixty seconds to run into a burning building and get something you hold valuable what would that thing be?" Even when you are considering tangible things that you could take it is quite a challenge to come up with a satisfactory answer. When you consider something as intangible as personal values, it is extremely tough to identify which value you really would not want to be without.

The answer to that question varies from person to person, but when you find that your spouse would 'grab' something different than you, it can cause conflict. It can also cause you to question their priorities.

- What would your answer be?

- Was your spouse's answer similar?

21

As you go through this journey of discovery together, don't fall into the trap of criticising your partner's values. Instead, take the time to ask deeper questions about why they feel that way or why something is important to them. Give them time to process and articulate their answers. Some of the things you will be discussing are issues that neither of you has put much thought into before. Be gracious to one another.

As a married couple, you share an incredible journey together, but you do not share the same brain. You have to flow together and in order to do that effectively, you will need to learn how to navigate your cross-cultural marriage. I like what 1 Peter 3:7 has to say: "LIKEWISE, HUSBANDS, LIVE WITH YOUR WIVES IN AN UNDERSTANDING WAY." That requires getting to know one another. Understanding and accepting each other rather than wanting to 'correct' one another.

KNOW YOU ARE UNIQUE ...
THAT MEANS YOUR SPOUSE IS TOO.
NOTICE THAT YOU HAVE VALUES YOU PRIORITISE ...
YOUR SPOUSE DOES TOO.
OBSERVE THAT YOU HAVE A UNIQUE PERCEPTION OF THE WORLD ...
YOUR SPOUSE DOES TOO.
WONDER AT THE MIRACLE OF YOUR UNIQUENESS ...
YOUR SPOUSE SHOULD TOO!

"You are the only you God made...
God made you and broke the mold."

Max Lucado, Cure for the Common Life: Living in Your Sweet Spot

WHERE DOES YOUR UNIQUE CULTURE COME FROM?

Wherever you live, you will carry your value system with you. Your values have been ingrained into you so they run deep and are difficult to change. Have you ever heard your spouse say, "You're just like your mother!" or "You're exactly like your dad"? Have you ever been guilty of stereotyping your spouse to the culture they come from? If you have then, you have probably identified parts of a value system they inherited. If you want to get below the surface, though, you will have to be willing to dig a little deeper.

A sociologist called Morris Massey identified three significant periods of time in which your values are established. As you read through these different stages, try and determine the values that you decided to embrace and those you decided to reject. It isn't enough for you to understand what makes you who you are. Make sure you take the time to share with your spouse! This is an excellent opportunity to grow together and share your lives.

The Imprint Period.

Aristotle said, "Give me a child until he is 7 and I will show you the man." This is the time when people learn to identify the difference between good and bad, right and wrong. Since this period is up to the age of seven, it is safe to assume that most of this information comes from parents. It is often a time of blind acceptance. A child accepts the established code of behaviour and is taught to conform to the model with which they have been presented. You may not consider this to be of much importance however it is generally agreed that this is a vital period in which children develop their values.

Roy and I had very different childhood experiences. The biggest contrast was in matters of faith. In my home we never missed a church service, it wasn't purely religion it was all about relationship. My parents modelled serving God and as a family, we knew that God came first no matter what. I have vivid memories of my parents leading family prayer and Bible study at home. It wasn't just 'Sunday' religion, relationship with Christ was part of our everyday lives. As a result of their dedication, I gave my life to Jesus at a very young age.

Roy, in contrast, grew up in an atheistic home. Christianity was viewed as a crutch for the weak and life was certainly not about serving God and serving others. His Sundays were spent either doing his own thing or spending time with family. Church was never a consideration. We had two very different imprint periods.

- What were you like as a young child?

- Was your spouse's experience similar?

- What 'stamp' did early childhood leave on you?

If your childhood was difficult or traumatic, ask your spouse to pray for you. If you sense that there are deeper issues that need to be dealt with make sure you find a counsellor who can offer you appropriate help.

The Modelling Period.

From age 8 until 13 we continue to observe the values which are modelled for us by our parents, other family members and also by other people of influence such as teachers. Blind acceptance gives way to a more discerning assessment of whether something is really of value. During this stage what adults say is judged on the merits of what they also do.

I found it difficult to remember back to this phase of

my life. I thought about the teachers I had in school but honestly struggled to remember their names never mind what impact they had on me. I then tried to think of other areas of my life where I may have been influenced by someone in authority. I suddenly remembered sitting in church on a hard pew and looking up at my Sunday School teacher.

I was surprised that this was the teacher I recalled. This lady was not young, she was not trendy, in fact, she was what I considered quite old. It is very possible that, in reality, she was probably the age I am now. Age is all relative! This lady would faithfully come and teach our Sunday School class.

One thing that we had to do in preparation for that class was to learn Bible verses, I don't mean a single memory verse, I mean whole chunks of scripture! Saturday evenings were often spent going over the verses and making sure we were ready for the next morning.

Edna (my Sunday School teacher) was often met with complaints from her students regarding her insistence that we needed to learn so much. Her usual response was that it was important. We were told that we shouldn't take for granted having a Bible and that the Word of God needed to be in our hearts not just on a page. She would tell us stories of people behind the iron curtain who didn't have that luxury.

One particular Sunday stands out in my memory. A student protested that the requirement to learn so much was like asking her to memorise Psalm 119, all 176 verses of it! I think we were all surprised when she didn't say much but merely gave a curt nod.

The following week Edna was already waiting for us when we sauntered into Sunday School. She asked us to sit down and open our Bibles. This was an unusual occurrence because the beginning of the lesson usually involved us reciting Bible verses. She told us to turn to Psalm 119 and with that, she closed her own Bible. She recited the whole thing, word perfect! At the end of her delivery she simply stated, 'It's important to learn the Word of God'. She modelled what she required of us. That message stayed with me, and I put it into practice. Verses often come back to memory just when I need the reminder that God is with me. I am thankful for her example.

When I look back, I find it hard to remember other things that impacted me in that 8-13-year-old period of my life as much as she did. I remember that lady not because of her fashion sense or because she was fun but because she had a deep conviction. Edna White is no longer alive, but her legacy is.

As you answer these questions remember the primary influencers during this period are usually parents, family, teachers or someone with authority.

- Who or what impacted you most during this period of your life?

- Share about one person who was a positive influence on your life.

- Share about one person who made an adverse impact on your life.

THE SOCIALISATION PERIOD.

This period, between the ages 14 to 21, is when our peers are the people of most influence. Sometimes people will try to break away from earlier instilled values and move towards those presented in the media or those that their friends uphold. Parents can get very frustrated during this period of transition, and if your socialisation period overlaps with time spent in another country, this can be blamed on what will be perceived as negative influences from another culture.

At age nineteen Roy stood on the platform of Rhyl train station waiting for an adventure to begin. He had his life bundled together in a camouflage-coloured rucksack that strained at the seams. Everyone thought that he was mad to be thinking about studying in Northern Ireland. It wasn't on the list of the 'hottest' places to visit. Unless of course, you were of the mindset that, going to a troubled country was appealing.

At that time Northern Ireland was hitting the news for all the wrong reasons, it was a beautiful country but tainted by terrorism. He wasn't exactly going there as his first choice either but he had received an offer to do an Aeronautical Engineering Degree at Queen's University Belfast, so he put his rucksack on his back and left home.

Faith seemed to be the centre of every conversation even if he was speaking to people who were unsure of theirs. From the boat journey over to the first weeks on campus religion naturally came up in conversations. Roy's lack of faith made him curious about the faith of others, and he took it upon himself to educate his new friends about their unfounded beliefs. The problem, however, was that Roy didn't have the expertise to counter their arguments and feeling ill-equipped he went to a bookstore and bought a Bible so he could argue more effectively. Friends equipped with faith, not just knowledge puzzled him.

This new season, new connections and new friendships became an influential voice in his life. In his socialisation period, his worldview changed, and he embraced beliefs far from his original culture.

It is important to recognise that you are not just

a clone of your parents. Many things have influenced your views along the way. Since no two people have identical experiences or reactions, you will have a different approach to life, your 'personal' culture.

So how is all of this relevant to you? Most cross-cultural couples will already have a firmly established set of values before they even meet. Those values are deeply ingrained and as such they are difficult, but not impossible, to change. For those who get married early and are still in the socialisation period blending together is usually a little easier than for those who are older. Having said that if you are both aware of the need to change the experience doesn't need to be a painful one.

- Which peers influenced you the most?

- Did that cause you to break away from any of your parents' beliefs?

- Have your parents blamed your spouse for any of the changes they see in you?

I have already mentioned that Roy and I had very different experiences growing up and as such our value systems were very different. Below are just a few of the contrasts in our upbringing:

Third Culture Kid versus Mono Culture Kid.

When we met, Roy had already lived in England, Australia, and Wales. Although my family had travelled abroad on holiday, I had lived most of my life in a small village called Loughgall and moved to the 'big town' when I was fifteen. I was very limited in my worldview or even geographical knowledge. To be quite honest I didn't know what I was getting myself into when I said 'I do' because I had a very limited understanding of cultural differences.

Atheist versus Christian.

Roy grew up in a home where religion was looked down upon. There was a certain degree of pride in being a 'heathen' and atheism was valued as the intelligent choice. Although Roy became a Christian in his late teens, we didn't share the same experiences or values when we were growing up.

I found myself falling into the trap of trying to be Roy's spiritual mentor and teaching him when I should have been concentrating on being his wife. Even if you are both Christian but have two different 'faith' backgrounds, it can impact your interaction with each other and also the way in which you choose to raise your children.

Single parent versus intact family.

At the tender age of seven Roy returned from Australia to the UK with his mum and brother. He didn't see his father again until he was in his twenties. While he grew up with an absent father, I grew up with my father's love and protection. Some of our struggles as a couple came from the fact that I had expectations of how a husband should treat his wife (e.g. my father frequently brought my mother flowers) and Roy didn't have that example.

Independent versus Interdependent.

I'm sure that growing up in Northern Ireland influenced the way in which my family interacted with one another. Although I only have one brother I have a big enough family network to make even a Greek proud. Celebrations were always shared with family; problems were shared with family. We weren't all dependent on one person; rather we relied on each other. I had no issue asking for help if a need arose, or helping others if they had something they needed a hand with.

In Roy's family independence was valued, being self-sufficient and self-reliant were important. He learned to do a lot by himself; he would consult a book and learn what he needed to learn to get the job done. It broke a value code to ask others for help even though he was more than willing to step up to the plate when anyone else needed something. Asking for help is something he still finds difficult today.

Spending versus Saving.

Although Roy's mum certainly knew how to save, when Roy moved into the socialisation period he learned how to spend. He had an 'I want it now; I'll buy it', mentality. Getting into debt was not something that concerned him so he had a tendency to impulse buy.

I had an 'I want it so I'll save for it' mindset. 'Save, save, save', been drummed into me by my parents from a very early age. Instead of impulse buying, I had been encouraged to walk away and think about whether I really 'needed' that thing. 'Wants' or 'wishes' were something that could be fulfilled either through saving or for a birthday or Christmas present. Roy viewed my tendencies as too 'tight' or frugal, and I saw his mindset as wasteful.

Take time now to identify some of the differences in the way you approach life.:

- Is either of you a T.C.K. (Third Culture Kid)?

- What is your faith background?

- What is your family background?

- Are you from an interdependent, dependent, or independent family?

- What is your attitude to money?

- Is it the same as your family's?

- Are there any other areas in which you can identify distinct differences?

Sometimes as Roy and I would try to work through these value differences, it would resemble two cymbals clanging together. There was a lot of noise but no give on either side. When you value something, you consider it to be of worth and as something of worth you will tend to guard it. Both of us stood guard over things we believed were important, and we came to an impasse.

- How have you worked through your value differences in the past?

- Are there areas of impasse?

- Which areas causes the most challenges?

When you find yourself at an impasse, go to 1 Corinthians 13. Real progress is made when you choose to love one another despite your differences. Love will remove the barriers.

The Way of Love

If I speak in the tongues
of men and of angels,
but have not love, I am a noisy gong or a clanging cymbal.
And if I have prophetic powers, and understand all mysteries and all knowledge, and
if I have all faith, so as to remove mountains, but have not love,

I am nothing.

If I give away all I have,
and if I deliver up
my body to be burned,
but have not love,
I gain nothing.

Love is patient

and kind; love does
not envy or boast;
it is not arrogant
or rude. It does not
insist on its own way;
it is not irritable
or resentful; it does

not rejoice at
wrongdoing, but
rejoices with the truth.
Love bears all things,
believes all things,
hopes all things,
endures all things.

Love never ends.

1 Corinthians 13:1-8 (ESV)

Your Unique Marriage

WOVEN TOGETHER

Over the last few chapters, we have focused on your uniqueness. Your similarities and your differences. While it's important to be aware of these, it's also important to understand another truth about marriage. It's incredible to think that with all the other relationships that we experience; parental relationships, relationships with your siblings, relationships with your friends, no other relationship promises what marriage does. In Genesis God explains the process of marriage, the process of two becoming one.

For this reason, a man shall leave his father and his mother,
and shall be joined to his wife;
and they shall become one flesh.
Genesis 2:24

In Genesis we see something take place which instead of focusing on the differences concentrates on two people coming together. God uses the term 'one-flesh' to help us understand what it means to be married. Marriage requires being willing to let go of the old to embrace the new! You need to allow Him to 'join' you together.

Psalm 139 describes us being 'knit together' body, soul and spirit. We have been formed by God's design. Many years ago I decided to learn how to embroider; each stitch took concentration, and every thread had to be carefully chosen. This Psalm uses this imagery to help us understand the care and attention God used when He created us. We truly have been 'embroidered with various colours'.

Culture isn't just one thread woven into us which defines our identity. Culture is also like the dye into which each thread has been dipped. The depth of that dye also varies from individual to individual. The strength to which you hold your beliefs and values will differ from someone else born and bred in the same culture. That dye contributes to your unique characteristics and impacts your character and how it is formed. It's a dye that isn't just surface level but rather one that runs deep. Often it can't be defined by tangible things like the foods you like or the clothes you wear because it is so much more than what you do.

Culture is part of you; it is who you are. That is why dealing with culture is often so emotive. When someone criticises your culture you take it personally, you feel like they are criticising you. Defensiveness is especially common in cross-cultural relationships, but it is not healthy.

#MARRIAGETIP

"Preservation of one's own culture does not require contempt or disrespect for other cultures."

Cesar Chavez

If you discover you are offending your spouse, examine how you speak about their home country, language and culture. Even if your loved one jokes about their own people group, it is likely that you do not have the license to do the same thing! Likewise, if you find yourself getting offended by your spouse examine the reasons why you are feeling offended. Does it have a cultural root?

- Are you guilty of disrespecting your spouse's culture?
- If so ask their forgiveness.

A cross-cultural marriage can be a rich tapestry if you allow yourselves to be woven together by God. It will take time; it will take patience it will take flexibility, but it can be a thing of great beauty when you allow God to choose the threads and work them together. We need to learn to celebrate the differences, embrace the contrasts and learn how to blend together. That may sound very poetic but being woven together can sometimes seem like a messy experience, the process often doesn't look pretty.

When your marriage looks ugly, remember that there are two sides to every tapestry, when it is woven there is a 'warp' side and a 'weft' side. The weft side is the side that will be visible in the finished work; it's the side that looks beautiful with the threads lying side by side in perfect harmony. The warp side is the side that will be hidden. While the transition may seem smooth on the surface, the warp side shows where the threads have been joined together.

Corrie Ten Boom is famous for preaching with a piece of cloth. She would speak about God's faithfulness and hold up the piece of cloth to illustrate. She always held it up the wrong way round as she talked about the difficulties she had encountered. The back of the cloth looked ugly and knotted, and it is hard to make out what it was. Then she would flip the cloth to reveal a beautiful embroidered crown. Few of us will encounter any difficulties that are even close to what she walked through in her life. Corrie learned to view things from God's perspective.

"Although the threads of my life have often seemed knotted,
I know, by faith,
that on the other side of the embroidery
...There is a Crown."

Corrie Ten Boom

The problem we can face in cross-cultural marriage is taking too close a look at the warp side of the process and becoming discouraged. It may be impossible to hope for a beautiful outcome when you are working at blending together. Don't allow the enemy to warp your view. It is important to have a vision of the finished product, not just the present circumstances. Cross-cultural marriages can be beautiful especially when you allow yourselves to be woven together by God's skilful hands.

I love the word in Hungarian for the promises and commitment a married couple make to one another; the word is szövetség. The translation is a covenant or union, but the literal translation is to be woven together. It truly expresses the miracle of this very special covenant that God designed.

While marriage can be viewed from different perspectives; some looking at it as just a piece of paper, and yet others taking the commitment incredibly seriously, it is important to see marriage the way that God designed it. Culture will not give us an accurate picture of this, to understand marriage we need to go back to the blueprint, the Word of God.

- Do you have a tendency to view the warp or the weft side of your relationship?

- Ask God to help you see His bigger plan instead of focusing on the negative.

- Have you found it easy to be woven together or are you finding yourselves tied in knots?

for marriage.

Flowing Together

Confluence is the name given in geography to when two bodies of water come together. Although the word is used when a tributary might join a larger river, I really like its other use. 'Confluence is when two streams join and become the source for a new river with a new name'. This is the definition of confluence that I feel most relates to marriage, two people who choose to start a new family, two people choosing to follow God's plan and become one.

Matthew 19:6 NIV
So they are no longer two, but one flesh.
Therefore what God has joined together,
let no one separate."

No two streams travel the same path; none have the same experience. The earth the streams have passed over may be smooth or rocky; the soil may be a different hue and the path for one may have been straight while for another it may have had many twists and turns. Confluence (or con-flux) can be seen in any marriage but in a cross-cultural marriage, the contrasts can be the most dramatic. When you learn how to flow together, your marriage can also be incredibly beautiful.

There are many images of confluence which show

the dramatic contrast that can be seen between two streams or rivers which join. The confluence of the Jialing and Yangtze Rivers in Chongqing in China or the confluence of the Green and Colorado Rivers in Canyonlands National Park, Utah, USA show the beauty and wonder of this process. Even with these natural wonders, and the ability to see two distinct rivers within one, they would be impossible to separate! God sees us the same way. He has joined us together. He views us as one.

Confluence isn't only a noun it is a verb; it describes the act or the process of merging. As you work on your marriage, don't focus only on where the water is churned up but step back and see the wonder of the bigger picture. Confluence in marriage might be a bit messy especially in the beginning, but you will learn to flow together. Too many couples see the turbulence in their relationship and divorce within the first year. They don't realise it is a process.

Tony and Anneke almost didn't survive their first year of marriage. They both thought they had made a major mistake. The novelty of married life wore off almost before the honeymoon was over when they discovered more than expected about each other. Strangely it wasn't anything major; there were no deep dark secrets or confessions of sin. They just didn't know how to live together.

Tony was surprised that Anneke did not serve him as he had expected. His mother wasn't perfect, but she was mindful of her role, and his father had no complaints. Anneke couldn't believe that Tony wasn't being considerate, wasn't picking up after himself, expected her to do so much. When she expressed her disappointment she was shocked when he told her that she was a disappointment too.

Neither of them had really thought much past the wedding day. It hadn't been so difficult to plan and organise the wedding but on reflection Tony expected that to be Anneke's role. It was a shock to the system to realise that married life wasn't running so smoothly. Both their expectations had been high, they both thought they had found the perfect catch which heightened their feelings of being let down.

IF YOU ARE NOT YET MARRIED:

- How do you envisage the confluence process?

- Do you expect it to be pretty smooth or quite turbulent?

- What do you anticipate the biggest 'adjustment challenge' will be when you get married?

- Are there areas you already find challenging with each other's culture?

- Have you discussed what your expectations of each other are in married life?

- How was your first year together as a couple?

- Were there any areas which caused turbulence between you?

- Were your expectations of your cross-cultural marriage accurate?

- How difficult do you find it to see the beauty in each other's cultures?

If there are areas of unforgiveness between you, take some time to forgive each other. Disappointments are destructive, ask God to give you realistic expectations of each other.

You might be wondering if there are ways to make confluence easier. Does it really have to be that turbulent, that traumatic? Here are some things you can put in place to make life easier and flow together well.

1. Communicate with a view to blending rather than holding your position.

2. Recognise that you will not just lose something you will gain in the process.

3. Remember, if you both give you both gain.

NAVIGATING YOUR CROSS-CULTURAL MARRIAGE

Driving on the Wrong Side of the Road.

Now we move from rivers to roads. Driving is one of those mundane things in life. It is part of our routine; it is something we rarely think about. Once you have gone through the learning process, you simply do it. My husband and I both learned to drive in the UK. I learned to drive in Northern Ireland, and he learned to drive in England. Driving on the left side of the road felt natural, it felt right. When we first moved to the U.S.A. and encountered the highway system there, everything felt wrong. I remember my first experience driving on the 'wrong' side of the road, everything inside me was screaming that I was going the wrong way and would probably crash. Navigating junctions was even more traumatic. Driving on the right is wrong … right?

During our time in Denver driving on the right got more comfortable I started to relax. My knuckles were no longer white as I gripped the wheel and I learned to drive on automatic pilot. I no longer had to brace myself coming up to a junction. I was confident, I knew what to do, and this was now natural.

Moving to the Hungarian road system wasn't necessarily a breeze. I had to learn to deal with, what I considered as, reckless drivers who thought nothing about overtaking at high speeds on narrow country lanes. Even though re-adjusting to narrower roads and a more aggressive driving style was challenging it had certainly helped to have had time driving on the right-hand side of the road before we made that move. It gave me one less thing to worry about.

Now, when we go back to the U.K. I frequently find myself getting in the driver's side of the car when I am not the one driving. If I am driving, I find myself reaching for the gear stick with the wrong hand. Driving in the U.K. is un-natural now and yet at one time it felt like that was the only correct way to drive.

So, why focus on driving? Well, as you have probably guessed, it isn't to prepare you to operate a car in a foreign country. This emphasis on the challenges of learning new road rules is something I hope will help you remember a fundamental principle as you navigate life with your spouse. Adjustment takes time. Time is something you can't hurry; you can't change the pace. When things are taking time, remember there are things you are struggling with at the moment that will begin to feel natural as you persevere.

As you live life together, you recognise there will be things your spouse does that you see as fundamentally wrong. Often that is not the case, be willing to look at things from a different perspective. Don't label things as wrong just because they are not what you are used to.

"But the key to our marriage is the capacity to give each other a break. And to realise that it's not how our similarities work together; it's how our differences work together."
Michael J. Fox

Different is Just Different It's Not Wrong

This simple revelation made a huge difference in our lives. It is a lesson we both wish we had learned early in our marriage. Sometimes we treat something as a sin which is simply different. It may feel intrinsically wrong because of our upbringing, but that doesn't mean it is actually wrong. We should talk about countries driving on the right side of the road or the left side, but I rarely hear people talk that way. They usually express it as 'they drive on the wrong side of the road'. We can fall into the trap of feeling the same way about culture if we don't just recognise that something can simply be different rather than wrong.

Our revelation of this fact came when we were sitting in a cross-cultural seminar in Missionary Training International near Colorado Springs. They were preparing us to move country and taught us strategies to deal with the challenges we would be facing. For Roy and I the principle "Different is just different it's not wrong" started to sink in. We realised though that while it was relevant to our move to Hungary, it was even more relevant to our marriage. The man sitting beside me wasn't wrong; he wasn't weird, and he wasn't strange, he was Roy, and he simply had a different culture than I did. Roy equally felt that it was like a light bulb had been switched on illuminating why we had been experiencing confusion and miscommunication.

> "WHEN MEN AND WOMEN ARE ABLE TO RESPECT
> AND ACCEPT THEIR DIFFERENCES
> THEN LOVE HAS A CHANCE TO BLOSSOM."
> JOHN GRAY

- Do you respect your spouse and their culture?

- Do you appreciate and value your spouse's opinion?

- Are there things you have considered to be 'wrong' about the way in which your spouse acts?

- Are they actually wrong (sinful) or are they just cultural?

If your answer is cultural, then you need to accept that your spouse has a different way of doing things. You will have to learn to reach agreement about what your 'new' culture will look like.

If your answer is sinful, then we'll address that in 'A CROSS-cultural Versus a Cross-cultural Marriage'. There are times when different can be wrong.

Changing the Rules of the Road

There is an old Irish joke that the Irish finally saw the light and decided to modify the road rules. They thought it was a huge transition to change from driving on the left to driving on the right so they decided to phase it in gradually.

While we will tackle the subject of humour a little later in the book, this joke hits home an important point about the merging of two cultures; there are likely to be some crashes along the way. We talk about blending and mixing cultures, and that may sound like quite a smooth process, but sometimes we find that a couple butts their heads together and can't understand why the other one doesn't give way.

Changing the rules of the road will not happen overnight. Some patterns will change naturally over time; others will take a deliberate decision to bring transformation. You have to work together to write a new Highway Code, one that will work for both of you. In fact, it is critical that you do!

A quick glimpse at a Highway Code book, especially if like me you haven't looked at one in a while, may surprise you. There are lots of rules about how to read signs, how to treat pedestrians, about passengers and weather conditions. As you work on your marriage, you will also need to learn how to navigate various situations. You may have to work out what to do when in-laws come to visit, how to be hospitable, how to reach agreement about parenting; but both of you get to decide. It isn't just about one person having to throw away their Highway Code and adopt another; it is about you writing a new book together.

You need to take it seriously! What will happen if two drivers, from countries with different road rules, insist on driving only with consideration to their rules? The answer is obvious! They will inevitably crash. What will happen if you both insist only on doing things your way?

- What topics cause the most 'crashes' in your relationship?

- Which of the following has been your approach to reaching agreement?

  - Playing chicken? (stubbornly holding on to your position hoping the other one will cave in first).

  - Driving erratically? (letting emotions take the wheel).

  - Pressing the accelerator? (adding other issues to the discussion to prove your point).

  - Slamming on the breaks? (You refuse to discuss the subject, slam on the brake and walk away).

  - Letting God take the wheel? (You stop and pray about it together and ask God for guidance).

My Way or the Highway

One of the biggest arguments Roy and I have ever had took place in a car. I don't remember much about the content of the argument although I do remember it had something to do with a lawnmower. Roy was driving, and I was in the passenger seat, and when the discussion started, it quickly escalated to a heated debate. Roy, as if punctuating his point with an exclamation mark, slammed on the brakes and pulled to the side of the road. Neither of us would give up our point of view, and Roy exited the car in anger.

I was left sitting in the passenger seat watching in the wing mirror, as Roy strode off into the distance, while I was left wondering what to do now. The problem was that we were both stubborn, both opinionated, both hard headed. We both intrinsically believed that we were the only ones with the right answer and it came down to it being 'my way or the highway'. We both wanted the other to change but wouldn't even consider changing ourselves.

We had fallen into something called ethnocentrism. Ethnocentrism is the belief that one's 'own' culture is in-finitely superior to others. It is one of the biggest threats to a cross-cultural marriage because those with this belief system will automatically treat their spouse as an inferior. Some guilty of ethnocentrism are completely ignorant that they are behaving in this way. To them, their way of doing things is simply the most logical, the only right and proper way. Their cultural value system is so ingrained that they are unable to see things from another point of view. Ethnocentrism boils down to pride.

God provides an antidote for ethnocentrism by enabling us to blend together, but it isn't something that happens magically. Blending together also only happens when we choose to blend.

COMPLETE MY JOY BY BEING OF THE **SAME MIND,**
HAVING THE **SAME LOVE,** BEING IN **FULL ACCORD** AND OF **ONE MIND.**
DO NOTHING FROM SELFISH AMBITION OR CONCEIT,
BUT **IN HUMILITY** COUNT OTHERS
MORE SIGNIFICANT THAN YOURSELVES.
LET EACH OF YOU **LOOK** NOT ONLY TO HIS OWN INTERESTS,
BUT ALSO **TO THE INTERESTS OF OTHERS.**

PHILIPPIANS 2:2-4

Philippians encourages the church to come into full accord with each other. Full accord doesn't only mean to agree but to completely agree. Strong's concordance defines the word phroneo as: "to be of the same mind i.e. to be agreed together, to cherish the same views, to be harmonious".

- Which part of being in full accord with each other do you struggle with the most?

  - Agreement?

  - Cherishing the same views?

  - Giving up pride?

  - Being harmonious?

It's important not to abandon the verse at this point. It goes on to say "Do nothing from selfish ambition or conceit, but in humility count others more significant than yourselves."

Marriage can quickly turn into a competition if we are not careful. If there is something that you are talking through, check your motives. Do you just want to win an argument or do you really feel strongly about the issue that you are discussing?

If you are going to have a competition in marriage then why not take up the Romans 12:10 challenge? It's a healthier rivalry.

> LOVE ONE ANOTHER WITH BROTHERLY AFFECTION.
> OUTDO ONE ANOTHER IN SHOWING HONOUR.
> ROMANS 12:10 (ESV)

Paul also tells us that it is important to lay aside conceit. Egotism will not be your ally in building a healthy marriage rather it will be your enemy. Narcissism is something that is on the increase; humility, however, is an entirely opposite mindset, and it is something we need to cultivate. Instead of approaching your spouse with the attitude of 'teaching' them how to do things right consider things from their point of view, think about what you can learn from them. You might be surprised to find that from their perspective and in the context of their culture their actions are entirely logical too. "Let each of you look not only to his own interests, but also to the interests of others" Philippians 2:4 is in total contrast from the "My way or the highway" mentality. It rebukes the Bridezilla's who use the 'my day, my way' mantra. It challenges the egotistic groom who demands submission.

It's important to purpose to change. Unfortunately, many people fail to alter their behaviour even when there is overwhelming evidence that it is destructive. You would think, for example, if someone was so ill that they needed heart bypass surgery they would change their eating and exercise patterns. Amazingly only 10% of those with that critical condition are willing to modify the way they live. Most continue with their normal lifestyle just hoping things will improve.

Most marriage issues are heart-related. You have a choice to make the lifestyle changes needed to have a healthy marriage, but it does take effort. You must be willing to change! It's necessary to get rid of the 'My way or the highway!' mentality. The good news is that we aren't reliant on our own will power or our own strength!

AND I WILL GIVE YOU A NEW HEART,
AND A NEW SPIRIT I WILL PUT WITHIN YOU.
AND I WILL REMOVE THE HEART OF STONE FROM YOUR FLESH
AND GIVE YOU A HEART OF FLESH.
EZEKIEL 36:26 ESV

- Have you had a 'My way or the Highway' mentality?

- Are you in need of a new 'heart' towards your spouse?

- Are you willing to make the changes necessary to enable you to take the journey called marriage together?

Alternative Routes

During our missionary training, we were told a story about a missionary who went to one of the African nations. This missionary was frustrated by the attitude he saw the village men display towards their wives. Used to walking hand in hand with his wife and felt that the village men lacked affection, a problem he decided to address.

The next day he confidently challenged the village chief about the practice of walking ahead of the woman when walking through the jungle. "I've noticed that when the village men walk through the jungle with their wives, they always walk in front. It's not right that they should make their wives take such a subservient position. Their behaviour is so arrogant! In my culture, we walk beside our women, hand in hand, as it should be."

The old chief smiled and shook his head and quickly corrected the missionary, a man walking in front of his wife was not arrogance rather he was placing his wife in the position of importance. The man was offering her his protection! Only a selfish and cowardly man would walk beside his wife or let his wife take the lead. In the jungle they could never be sure what threat they would meet; the man was willing to sacrifice himself to keep his wife safe.

The missionary learned a valuable lesson that day. He was judging the behaviour of the village people on the basis of his own culture's customs. He had assumed the men's motive, and he had been wrong.

Perspective can change everything. Interpreting other's actions through your own culture will not enhance your understanding because it probably won't seem logical when it is taken out of context. Looking at the situation from their perspective will help you make great strides towards deepening your relationship.

If either of you finds something in you which is rooted in arrogance or self-importance then it is important to repent, ask God for forgiveness, apologise and forgive each other. Ask God to help you put your spouse's needs before your own.

The threat of ethnocentrism may be more likely to come from your in-laws rather than your spouse. In a cross-cultural marriage, there is a certain inevitability that you will be formally introduced to this attitude whether you would like to meet it or not. It is often a shock to realise that, at times, it resides in you.

DO NOTHING FROM SELFISH AMBITION OR CONCEIT,
BUT IN HUMILITY COUNT OTHERS
MORE SIGNIFICANT
THAN YOURSELVES.

PHILIPPIANS 2:3 ESV

- Are there areas in your marriage where you have been blind to your spouse's perspective?

- Have you been guilty of ethnocentrism?

- If so ask forgiveness and ask God to help you change.

Letting God Take the Wheel

Jesus take the wheel
Take it from my hands
Cause I can't do this on my own
I'm letting go
So give me one more chance
Save me from this road I'm on
Jesus take the wheel

Carrie Underwood

You're probably reading this book because you have a sneaking suspicion there might be a better way to do things. Perhaps you have found a few places in your cross-cultural relationship where you have reached a dead end, and you aren't sure how to get on the right track. It might be that one of you has been steering, or both of you have been fighting over the steering wheel, but your marriage hasn't gone in the direction you had hoped.

*Trust in the Lord with all your heart,
and do not lean on your own understanding.
In all your ways acknowledge him,
and he will make straight your paths.
Proverbs 3:5-6 ESV*

To get your relationship on the right track, it's important that you let go of control. Proverbs tells us that we need to learn to trust God instead of our own understanding. This is certainly true in the area of marriage! It's important to acknowledge that God has a role in your relationship. He designed it and that it is time to follow his road map.

Stuart Mignon in his book Jesus Take the Wheel says this, "Who is at the wheel of your life? You can determine the answer to this question by determining who is in control of the things you value most (i.e. your children, job, finances, home, health and relationships, even your daily activities). Do you often worry about any of these areas? Worry is a signpost telling us that we are once again behind the wheel."

- Who is at the wheel of your marriage?

- Are you willing to give God full control?

A †-CULTURAL

VERSUS

A CROSS-CULTURAL

MARRIAGE

The Need for Change

Samuel L. Britten wrote a cross-cultural story which has become quite famous in cross-cultural training. It is about a group of people called the Roundheads who moved to a land inhabited by the Squareheads. The Squareheads thought the Roundheads looked weird and talked funny so, in time, the Roundheads changed so they would better fit the society around them. They couldn't fully become Square-heads, but they did their best and managed to change their head shape to be hexagonal. The Hex-heads (for that is what the Roundheads had become) still did not fully fit into the Squarehead culture, but they did their best to continue to adapt and change. One day the Hex-heads decided to re-turn to the land of the Roundheads only to find people who thought they looked weird and talked funny.

The story is used to illustrate adaptation from one culture to another. How the changes you go through will mean that you may not fit in the culture you originated from, nor will you fully fit in the culture to which you move. Since you are not truly one culture or the other culture you de-velop a third culture, hence the term Third Culture Kid used to describe missionary or ex-patriot children.

The third culture effect is present in every marriage. Once you say 'I do' you start to adapt and change to become more like one another. For some, this experience is difficult and painful, while others find it easy to adapt. In fact, you may not even be aware of the changes happening, but they become glaringly obvious when you go back to your parental home to visit. Family members may start to look at you as though you are a Hex-head, and they may not like it!

Accepting Change

Accepting change can be challenging, especially if you don't understand why there is a need for change. Even if you do grasp that you need to adapt it's hard to identify the areas in which transformation should take place.

On a basic cultural level, behavioural modifications often occur in the area of manners. You quickly realise what is considered unacceptable in your adopted country. You learn that you will not make friends and influence people if you are thought of as rude, so you learn the basic rules of asking for something in a way that society considers to be a polite manner.

There are transformations which are pretty neutral, old habits which fall away and new ones which are adopted. None of that change requires you to admit something from your culture is 'wrong'. There are occasions though when changes need to be made because something is wrong!

WHEN DIFFERENT IS WRONG

You may be thinking, "Wait a second! You said earlier that different was just different it's not wrong. Why do I need to change?" You're right! I did say that, but there are occasions when different can be wrong.

Culture teaches us that there are right ways and wrong ways to do things, the acceptable and the unacceptable. Culture reprimands us when we step outside of these rules. Culture reinforces that alternative behaviours are indeed wrong. As you filter behaviour through your 'ethical' glasses, you will view things as black and white.

Through 'ethical' glasses clear boundaries are visible. Stepping over those boundaries is considered as sinful. It is absolutely necessary though to take those 'glasses' off for a moment and ask yourself if that behaviour aligns with God's guidelines or not. Culture can say that God's 'right' is wrong and God's 'wrong' is right. We need to line up with what God says.

Don't assume that because your national heritage is Christian that your cultural behaviour will be on track. Many nations are Christian in name only; some are Christian in name, but erroneous teaching has crept in, and the culture is not aligned with God's plumb line. Neither are you asking yourself if the behaviour lines up with your Christian culture. You need to ask yourself if it lines up with the Word of God. There is a big difference between the two questions! In response you are going to get one of three answers, yes, it's a neutral issue or no.

- If the answer is yes it aligns with God's Word, then we need to accept it. In fact, we need to go even further than that and where possible implement it.

- If the answer is neutral, then there is still a Godly way to deal with any disagreements between the two of you regarding this behaviour. A CROSS-cultural way.

- If the answer is 'no it doesn't align with God's guidelines' then something has to change. When the answer is no this is when the 'Different is just different it's not wrong' doesn't stand up. There are times when different is wrong, and 'wrong' needs to change to 'right' by changing behaviour.

Two Extremes

Barnabas had been taught that he was the head of the home. As the head of the home, he should make sure he reinforced his authority over his wife. He hated it when she 'stepped out of line' because he knew the cultural expectation and he didn't like executing it. He did not feel comfortable with punishing his wife in this demeaning fashion; it didn't feel right. The elders had challenged him, in no uncertain terms, to teach his foreign wife to line up. Now he was in a predicament.

Faced with this challenge he felt prompted to pray and read the Bible. Surely there would be some answers to his situation. He needed to know for sure that what the elders said was correct if he was going to carry this through. They had quoted Ephesians 5:22 'Wives, submit to your own husbands, as to the Lord.' So he thought it was wise to start his search there.

He decided it was probably best to read the whole chapter and he was surprised by what he found. The first half said a lot about behaviour. It didn't just talk about the things to avoid doing; it addressed how to behave with other believers. What if this was also applied to how he should treat his wife, she was a believer after all. That varied significantly to the model he had seen in the home he grew up in.

In verse 25 he found something even more disturbing. Ephesians 5:25 'Husbands, love your wives, as Christ loved the church and gave himself up for her.' Why hadn't that been taught with the same force that submission was taught? Barnabas realised that something was wrong, what he had been told wasn't balanced.

...To Another

Lynsey wore the pants in the relationship. No one was in doubt about that! Certainly not her husband. She had taken charge right from the start and in no way wanted to relinquish control after all she could be trusted to make good decisions for the family. She was so sure about Thomas's abilities. It wasn't that she didn't love him, she did, but he hadn't the cultural awareness that she had. This country was her home turf, and she knew how things ticked.

She didn't realise that they were headed for problems until she started to see that Thomas was pulling away emotionally. He did what he was told when he was told, but she could tell that when he looked at her resentment had replaced the look of admiration. At first, she simply got irritated; this was the 21st century, after all! Women were bosses in the workplace; feminism had overthrown all that archaic headship and submission nonsense.

A few days later Lynsey sat at the kitchen table reading a note that Thomas had written. He couldn't take it anymore. He couldn't live with her disrespect. He couldn't take another one of her orders; he was a man, not a child! Didn't she realise that her behaviour wasn't Christian? Her first response was to scrunch up the note and toss it in the bin in a temper. A temper which she had used in the past to get her own way, she realised. She retrieved the note and read it again. Where had she gone wrong?

Lynsey was a Christian but had deliberately gone deaf to what she considered being a chauvinistic attempt to gain power over women. She decided that Thomas just needed to understand that times had changed, and his beliefs were outdated. She'd prove it to him!

She began her search for 'proof'. 'First to prove equality!', she thought. She was delighted with herself when she found this verse in the Bible.

For in Christ Jesus you are all sons of God, through faith.
For as many of you as were baptised into Christ have put on Christ.
There is neither Jew nor Greek, there is neither slave nor free,
there is no male and female, for you are all one in Christ Jesus.
And if you are Christ's, then you are Abraham's offspring,
heirs according to promise.
Galatians 3:26-29 (ESV)

Just as she was rubbing her hands together, she heard God speak to her. "Your relationship isn't equal, you've made yourself the boss".

Discomfort settled on her shoulders as she continued her search. There were some things she couldn't reconcile. How could men and women be equal and yet have different roles in their relationship? She knew she was missing something.

The Truth Between the Extremes

Too many times our beliefs go from one extreme to another. The truth has often been stretched to fit around a cultural mindset and when the truth has been stretched it is no longer the truth but a lie. This area is just one of many where misteaching has been present.

To truly understand what a CROSS-cultural marriage should look like you need to be willing to study. Approach it with an open mind rather than a closed one. Ask God to help you understand HIS truth about HIS plan for marriage.

The issue of headship and submission is just one of those 'hot topics' which often seems magnified when viewed in a cross-cultural context. It's vitally important to understand it correctly, or you will have an unhappy marriage. We'll take another look at this subject in the CROSS referencing section of this book.

- What are the 'hot topics' in your relationship?

- Are there issues where you find yourselves poles apart?

- Commit to studying to discover where the truth really lies.

When Different is Right

Remember the phrase I used before 'Different is just different it's not wrong'. While that holds true in a lot of situations in the cross-cultural marriage context it's also important to realise another truth: there are times when different is right. You've studied the Bible; you know that you are on track with God, but it sets you in opposition to the culture you were brought up in.

In 1 Peter 2:11 Christians are described as foreigners, exiles, temporary residents, sojourners or aliens. We all fall into that 'hex-head' category. The 'they look weird and talk funny' category that Samuel L. Britten wrote about. In a sense, we do need to get comfortable that we will never actually belong to culture, but we do belong to God (1 Corinthians 3:23).

Staying true to your beliefs if you live in a society which opposes them isn't easy. If you spend enough time in a culture, you start to take on the attributes and characteristics of those in that society. In 1 Peter 2:12 Peter doesn't tell us to blend in. He says, "Live such good lives among the pagans that, though they accuse you of doing wrong, they may see your good deeds and glorify God on the day he visits us."

The outside world, your adopted culture, your own culture and your own society will probably never 'get' you. Becoming very comfortable with that is important. You shouldn't bow to the pressure of 'culture' if what society says is contrary to the Word of God, instead Peter encourages living good or 'honourable' lives.

Everything about Roy flies in the face of the Hungarian Machoism Model. Think of a stereotypical image of a macho male. Someone who thinks men are just that little bit better, and thinks that gives them a right to special treatment. Unfortunately, it often means that women do not get treated with the respect that they deserve. Machoism isn't something which is isolated to Hungary; it's a worldwide problem.

It's actually quite difficult to be a godly man and take the flak for it. It might be mistaken for his 'English' ways, but Roy doesn't line up with the English culture either. There is a degree of Machoism in English culture too. Roy has worked hard to line up with God's Word, and he tries to follow Christ's example. That means he doesn't put me down; it means he loves me selflessly. I, of course, reap the benefits of his actions in our home, but I know it isn't easy to take a stand and be willing to differ from the cultural norm.

Don't copy the behaviour and customs of this world,
but let God transform you into a new person
by changing the way you think.
Then you will learn to know God's will for you,
which is good and pleasing and perfect.
Romans 12:2 NLT

Basically, we need a CROSS-culture. Becoming more like Christ. Here we are told not to try and fit into the pattern of this world. While we may make some adjustments that don't break our moral code (as outlined by God, not culture), we do need to focus on having a marriage based on God's culture rather than the culture we originate from. I love that Romans 12:2 gives us a valuable key to transition. "Let God transform you into a new person by changing the way you think".

Since our culture essentially is the way we have been conditioned to think it's easy to see why it's our thought life that needs to be transformed. That 'thinking' changes the more we spend time with God. It's God who can enable us to undergo a metamorphosis. Just as a culture can rub off on us if we spend a lot of time in it, we alter our behaviour as we spend time with Jesus.

In the Christian world, we often use the term conversion to describe the change that occurs in our hearts when we give our lives to Christ. To convert means to change, to transform, to refashion and reform. God is in the business of behavioural modification. He can help us get it right where we have been getting it wrong.

> AND WE ALL, WHO WITH UNVEILED FACES
> CONTEMPLATE THE LORD'S GLORY,
> ARE BEING TRANSFORMED INTO HIS IMAGE
> WITH EVER-INCREASING GLORY,
> WHICH COMES FROM THE LORD,
> WHO IS THE SPIRIT.
> 2 CORINTHIANS 3:18

Adapting to a cross-cultural marriage is so much easier if we are submitted to God and allow him to re-dip our 'cultural dye' in exchange for His.

- Do you recognise things which you are stubbornly holding onto even though they are sinful?

- Ask God to help you let go of those things and give you His identity.

CULTURAL
REFERENCING

Cultural Referencing

There are many things about cultures which are fantastic; they make our lives richer they also give us a sense of identity. Intrinsic to each culture is a moral code. Culture dictates what is right and wrong. Over the centuries this has caused confusion because culture often provides a moral compass but that compass can be out of alignment.

In practice, blending two cultures together can be a complicated process. Often one, or both spouses feel as though they have lost part of their identity. Where moral issues are involved, it becomes even harder to discern the right way forward.

In order to blend effectively, you need to stop thinking cross-culturally and think CROSS-culturally. Your focus needs to be on what Jesus says rather than on your culture's voice. If you both strive to have a marriage centred on Jesus then having a happy and healthy marriage is very attainable. This will require you to make a transition from cultural referencing to CROSS referencing

When faced with decisions you need to use the Bible as your plumb line. Don't hold back from asking the difficult questions. When you face a conflict in your relationship, the first question should be "Why am I defending this?" It's always good to double check what your motive is behind your actions. Sometimes we go into defence mode even if we don't have a true conviction that something is right or wrong. It may simply be that we don't like it when we don't get our own way. There are issues though which force us to ask a second question, "Has this situation anything to do with culture?"

If your reason for your conviction involves why your Dad wouldn't like something, why your mother wouldn't like something or why your Grandparents wouldn't like something then you could be dealing with something cultural.

For the longest time, I didn't feel comfortable knitting on a Sunday. It was like a 'sin' to me. Obviously, the Bible doesn't say anything about knitting so why did I have such a problem with it? However, my Grandmother did have an issue with it. She didn't like us knitting on Sunday. She would say "You'll pick out every stitch that you knit on a Sunday, with your nose, in hell". I think that she drew that conclusion because she considered knitting to be work. That was hardly surprising with a lot of children to clothe! She had firmly tucked knitting into a non-Sabbath day activity. Exodus 20:8 was the basis.

Knitting was recreation for me so it is hard to accept her edict. Even with the knowledge that knitting wasn't a sin, I lacked the freedom to go ahead and knit. Her voice (not the voice of the Holy Spirit) would echo in my mind every time I lifted a set of knitting needles on Sunday.

- Are there things which you feel strongly about which are wrong from a cultural reference point?

- Are you tempted to force these on your spouse or your family?

- Is there scriptural evidence for your conviction?

- Is that scriptural evidence sound?

✝-Referencing

CROSS-Referencing

All Scripture is breathed out by God and profitable for teaching, for reproof, for correction, and for training in righteousness, that the man of God may be complete, equipped for every good work.
2 Timothy 2:16-17

We need to study the Word, not the culture! While it's impossible to give a full lesson here on biblical hermeneutics it's important to say that study (and application), not just reading, is essential. Paul commended the Bereans in the book of Acts because they weren't gullible. They really wanted to learn. They didn't take on board everything they had been told without checking that it was true. They went back to the Scriptures to make sure that Paul wasn't lying to them. It's important that you do the same!

Now the Berean Jews were of more noble character than those in Thessalonica, for they received the message with great eagerness and examined the Scriptures every day to see if what Paul said was true.
Acts 17:11 (NIV)

What the Berean Jews did is what I call CROSS-referencing. Make sure you examine both the Old and the New Testament. Things change as they go through the cross. Some things become harder, and some things become easier as you CROSS-reference them. It's important to know what those are and especially in relation to your marriage.

Matthew 5:27-28 Is a good example. Jesus gives us a higher standard to live by. You have heard that it was said, 'Do not commit adultery.' But I tell you that anyone who looks at a woman to lust after her has already committed adultery with her in his heart. Matthew 5:27-28 (BSB)

Even more strongly Jesus says in verse 29 "If your right eye causes you to sin, gouge it out and throw it away. It is better for you to lose one part of your body than for your whole body to be thrown into hell."

It's interesting that we reject this verse. There aren't many people going around these days with a missing eye because it caused them to sin. Yes, it sounds ridiculous to suggest that this should even be a possibility. The thing is though that you shouldn't reject the deeper meaning behind the verse.

The point of this verse is to hate the sin, hate that part of our culture enough to reject it and turn away from it. Yet, many sit in front of a computer screen or a TV in their homes and dedicate hours to that portal which goes directly against Jesus' words. This is not exclusively referring to the viewing of pornography; there are many things people view which stimulate sexual arousal or cause lustful thoughts. Millions of spouses worldwide commit adultery on a daily basis and then wonder why their marriage isn't working. They conclude that something must be wrong with marriage when the reality is they aren't lining up with God's Word. Don't just study the Word of God, APPLY it!

If you want to have a CROSS-cultural marriage, then make sure you live by the Word of God rather than your culture's standards. It will cost you something, but it will be worth it.

You need to be purposeful and lay down preconceived ideas about a topic and search the scriptures together to find out the truth. If you discover that what has been ingrained in you is off-base, then don't defend your culture. Stop making excuses and instead, ask God to help you line up with His Word.

- Which one has had the loudest voice in your life cultural opinion or the Bible?

- Do you make it a habit to CROSS-reference what you hear?

- Do you spend time together as a couple praying and reading the Bible together?

- If you know there are areas of your life which don't line up with God's Word: Repent, ask God's forgiveness and ask your spouse for forgiveness also.

- Ask God to help you as you study and apply His Word to your life.

†- Referencing Customs

I stood with Roy at the door of the church as the photographer snapped photos of the happy event when the unexpected happened. My mother-in-law thrust into my hand a plastic chimney sweep on a long black ribbon and insisted I hold it 'for luck'. I had no idea what she was doing or why she was doing it. Now that I know more about the tradition I'm surprised she didn't pay a chimney sweep to show up and kiss me for luck. Before I could ask her what she was doing, she then presented me with a silver horseshoe on a white ribbon. She probably wondered why I wore a look of horror rather than one of joy. She'd given me 'good luck' after all.

I exchanged looks with Roy who was equally baffled. My dilemma was how to get rid of the ugly things without offending my mother-in-law. I also had to get rid of them quickly enough to not offend many of the guests, who like me did not believe in luck! I felt the irony as I stood on the steps of the church with the offending articles. I felt we were making contradictory statements: the first being that we trusted God with our marriage, the second being that somehow we needed 'fortune' to make it work.

Looking back, I couldn't have done anything differently. It hadn't even registered that I was entering a cross-cultural marriage. I had no idea that there would be a difference in expectations when it came to the wedding day. I was flying blind.

I am more than aware that those who read this book will fall into at least two categories. Those who are already married and might look back on their wedding day wishing some things could be done differently and those preparing for their big day. To the first group, there may be things you need to learn to laugh about, pray over, forgive each other for. To the second group be prepared. Do your research, find out about the customs and traditions you might be faced with. Decide together what you will allow and what you won't allow. Agree on how you will handle any situations if they arise. If you are going to offend someone, it is very likely that a wedding day is a prime occasion to do it.

Wedding customs can range from the bizarre to the ridiculous but how can you tell which are harmful and which are not? Which traditions should you embrace and which should you reject? In a cross-cultural marriage, there will be things that one of you considers reasonable while the other one might hate the thought.

A white wedding dress is one such example. For most of the West wearing white is a tradition while, in a lot of countries, the bride wears vibrant colours. A colour which many associate with mourning might seem really inappropriate in your spouse's culture. When Queen Victoria started the trend in 1840, she caused quite a stir for this very reason. When we got married, you could cause a stir if you chose not to wear white (which by then had become the symbol of purity). Cream, while more flattering for many brides, was to be avoided if you wanted to stop gossips jumping to conclusions.

For those planning their big day, or for in-laws involved in the getting ready for marriage here are a few helpful questions to ask yourself:

- Is the custom Godly or ungodly or neutral?

- Does it line up with scripture?

- Is there any occultic connection to the custom?

- Where did the custom originate?

- Does it still mean the same today or has the meaning changed?

- Is the tradition more important than the harmony of your relationship with your future family?

- By eliminating a custom, will the bride or groom still feel married if it is not part of the ceremony?

- What wedding traditions in your spouse's/spouse-to-be's culture do you find most difficult to accept?

✝- Referencing Love

The Universality of Love

Most languages have an expression which means, 'I love you'. Love has survived history; it has survived cultures it thrives even when surrounded by hate. Love is a phenomenon that defies understanding and is difficult to define. The understanding of what love is and how it is expressed can vary widely from culture to culture or from person to person. It is invisible and yet tangible.

Science points to the universality of love regardless of the cultural acceptance of romantic love. An article from the New York Times called 'Love on the Global Brain' points to research which confirms that 'Love' has the same effect on the brain even if society frowns on the concept. Social conditioning is unable to drown out Divine design. That doesn't surprise me at all! After all, we were made in God's image, and God is love.

Dr Gary Chapman wrote a book entitled 'The 5 Love Languages' which immediately gained traction because couples realised that there was a disconnect in how they were communicating love. It's clear that saying 'I love you' in whichever language you speak is not enough to clearly articulate that deep felt emotion. Love is a verb which needs to be demonstrated in words, attitudes and actions.

Love and Romance

Most women assume when the word 'action' is mentioned that the demonstration of love should be through romantic gestures. Most men assume it should be demonstrated by passion. Society has been bombarded by propaganda regarding 'true love' little of which takes into consideration the boring and mundane aspects of life. How many shows portray actions like washing the dishes or putting out the bins as loving gestures?

That isn't to say that romance should not be part of a relationship, it should! Romance is simply one expression of love, and it's good to find different ways to communicate that.

An illusion of love has been presented which makes many couples doubt if they are with the right person or if they should be searching for someone better. Yet, that is all that it is. It is an illusion. The reality is far removed from the fantasy lives presented to us on the big screen, in novels or through pornography. These false representations of love are counterfeits to the real thing.

Love by Design

Love is a gift, given by God. His Word is his love letter to us. In it, He explains how He loves us and offers us an example to follow. He doesn't leave us to blindly follow our emotions but instead teaches us how to build Godly character so our love can be sustained.

Love and the word passion often go hand in hand. There is an expectation not only of romance but sexual excitement.

Sexual fulfilment was certainly part of God's design for marriage, but there is another element of passion which we often miss.

Passion is a word that originates in Latin. Its meaning goes beyond the modern-day meaning of the word. The original meaning implied suffering and enduring. In other words, passion isn't all 'feeling', but it's commitment.

Ephesians 5:1-2 (ESV) tells us to 'walk in love', with Jesus as our example.

Therefore be imitators of God, as beloved children. And walk in love, as Christ loved us and gave himself up for us, a fragrant offering and sacrifice to God.

Jesus is the definition and the demonstration of love. He is the model we need to follow, a model of selflessness, an example of sacrificial love. The cross is the ultimate symbol of love.

JOHN 3:16 FOR GOD SO LOVED THE WORLD, THAT HE GAVE HIS ONLY SON, THAT WHOEVER BELIEVES IN HIM SHOULD NOT PERISH BUT HAVE ETERNAL LIFE.

The cost of genuine love is high; it requires sacrifice. The type of love that is sometimes missing in marriage is Agape Love. It's opposed to many of the models of love our cultures provide. It is counter-cultural and profoundly powerful.

Whether you got married to someone of your own choosing, or entered an arranged marriage God's expectation of you is the same. To love as He loves, to put your spouse's needs before your own.

When Love Has Boundaries

In some cultures, any cross-cultural marriage is perceived to be wrong, so wrong in fact that laws were made against it. This phenomenon has been particularly true of interracial marriages. The deeply held belief that many cultures have that marrying someone of another race is sinful is an important one to face. This is often based on ethno-centric beliefs rather than on a biblical basis. Acts 17:26

makes it clear that God created all the races and that all the ethnic backgrounds originated from Adam.

And he made from one man every nation of mankind to live on all the face of the earth, having determined allotted periods and the boundaries of their dwelling place. Acts 17:26 The following verse has often been used incorrectly as 'evidence' that interracial marriages are frowned on by God.

YOU SHALL NOT INTERMARRY WITH [THE NATIONS]; YOU SHALL NOT GIVE YOUR DAUGHTERS TO THEIR SONS, NOR SHALL YOU TAKE THEIR DAUGHTERS FOR YOUR SONS. DEUTERONOMY 7:3

Reading this verse in isolation you can see why. It seems clear, doesn't it? However, if you don't take this verse in isolation and read verse four you'll discover it isn't so cut and dried.

For they will turn your sons away from following Me to serve other gods; then the anger of the Lord will be kindled against you. Deuteronomy 7:4

Was it a warning about interracial marriage or a warning about not being led away from worshipping God? It isn't the purity of the races that is at threat; it is the purity of faith. This Old Testament warning carries into the New Testament.

DO NOT BE UNEQUALLY YOKED WITH UNBELIEVERS.
FOR WHAT PARTNERSHIP HAS RIGHTEOUSNESS WITH LAWLESSNESS?
OR WHAT FELLOWSHIP HAS LIGHT WITH DARKNESS?
2 CORINTHIANS 6:14 ESV

The light and darkness mentioned in this verse have nothing to do with the colour of someone's skin but everything to do with the condition of their heart. A yoke is representative of work; it also represents guidance and direction. Going through life taking the spiritual responsibility on your shoulders alone is difficult. In Genesis, we are told that one of the purposes of marriage is that we can help one another. Without both of you working together under the guidance of the Holy Spirit you will pull in different directions. You will be unequally yoked.

1 CORINTHIANS 7:39 NIV A WOMAN IS BOUND TO HER HUSBAND AS LONG AS HE LIVES. BUT IF HER HUSBAND DIES, SHE IS FREE TO MARRY ANYONE SHE WISHES, BUT HE MUST BELONG TO THE LORD.

It's a verse that gives freedom and yet sets limitations. It gives freedom of choice with only one stipulation. The person a Christian marries should be a Christian. In this verse, there is no limitation of culture, no boundary of ethnic background. Faith is the issue. It's a verse which pulls us back to the garden of Eden when Adam and Eve were given the freedom of choice from all of the trees in the garden but were given a limitation.

Paul addressed the issue of what to do if you find yourself in this situation i.e. married to a non-Christian. Whether that's because of making a choice which isn't biblical, or because they make a decision to become a Christian after they are married, the advice doesn't seem to change. 1 Corinthians 7:12-17 outlines what to do.

"To the rest I say this (I, not the Lord): If any brother has a wife who is not a believer and she is willing to live with him, he must not divorce her. And if a woman has a husband who is not a believer and he is willing to live with her, she must not divorce him. For the unbelieving husband has been sanctified through his wife, and the unbelieving wife has been sanctified through her believing husband. Otherwise your children would be unclean, but as it is, they are holy.

But if the unbeliever leaves, let it be so. The brother or the sister is not bound in such circumstances; God has called us to live in peace. How do you know, wife, whether you will save your husband? Or, how do you know, husband, whether you will save your wife?

Concerning Change of Status
Nevertheless, each person should live as a believer in whatever situation the Lord has assigned to them, just as God has called them. This is the rule I lay down in all the churches."

✝- Referencing Covenant

The Bible uses the word covenant to describe marriage. Don't assume that even if you both have used the word covenant to describe your commitment to one another that you both have the same understanding of what that means. Never assume you are both talking about the same thing just because you use the same word!

> "YOU KEEP USING THAT WORD,
> I DO NOT THINK IT MEANS WHAT YOU THINK IT MEANS."
> INIGO MONTOYA, THE PRINCESS BRIDE

Take some time now to talk about what you believe your commitment to each other is.

- Are there any 'deal breakers' in your viewpoint?

- How long does a covenant last?

- What's the difference between a covenant and a contract?

It may be that you have agreed about what covenant means to you but does it line up with what God means by covenant? Just as you should never assume you are both talking about the same thing because you use the same word, you should never assume that you know what God means because a word is familiar to you. Be willing to dive a little deeper and find out what He has to say in the correct context, the original language and in balance with other scriptures.

Just a piece of paper?

Some societies reject the idea of marriage and think that it is 'just a piece of paper'. They do not recognise it as anything other than a legal ceremony which contractually binds two people together. It's important to understand that a contract and covenant were not created equal. One was man's invention the other was God's. A contract is a piece of paper sealed by ink; a covenant is an agreement sealed by God.

A contract is conditional while a covenant is unconditional, 'For better, for worse, for richer, for poorer, in sickness and in health'. It covers all the bases! It not only outlines that you should live together but how you should live together. Most couples promise that they will love and cherish each other. That means taking an active part in making the marriage work.

A contract usually has a 'sell by date' in other words it expires after a certain length of time. A covenant lasts your entire lifetime. In the marriage covenant, part of the vows you make are 'until death us do part'. That's a lifetime guarantee! When you make your vows, they are stronger than you might think.

Mean What You Say.

When a man makes a vow to the LORD or takes an oath to obligate himself by a pledge, he must not break his word but must do everything he said.
Numbers 30:2 NIV

Only a few cultures remain today which value someone's word as highly as this implies. In years gone by a shake of the hand, a word, a spit, an exchange was enough to make a guarantee. A person's honour was at stake and the honour of their families if they did not keep their word.

- How highly valued is someone's promise in your culture?

- What is the condition of marriage in your society?

God's attitude towards vows and the words we speak is also seen in Ecclesiastes 5:5 NASB

When you make a vow to God, do not be late in paying it; for He takes no delight in fools. Pay what you vow! It is better that you should not vow than that you should vow and not pay. Do not let your speech cause you to sin and do not say in the presence of the messenger of God that it was a mistake. Why should God be angry on account of your voice and destroy the work of your hands?...

"I made a mistake getting married". This is a sentence we have repeatedly heard in our years of working with marriages. "I thought it was God's will, but it wasn't" is another variation of the theme. Yet, here we learn that God still expects vows to be kept.

- Has this changed the way you understand vows?

- What does this mean even if you feel your marriage was a mistake?

Do What You Promised

In the book of Malachi God makes it clear how he views the vows made in the marriage covenant. Unfortunately, there were consequences that Judah had to face for taking the vows he spoke so lightly.

"...This is another thing you do:
you cover the altar of the LORD with tears,
with weeping and with groaning,
because He no longer regards the offering
or accepts it with favour from your hand.
"Yet you say, 'For what reason?'
Because the LORD has been a witness
between you and the wife of your youth,
against whom you have dealt treacherously,

THOUGH SHE IS YOUR COMPANION
AND YOUR WIFE BY COVENANT.
"BUT NOT ONE HAS DONE SO
WHO HAS A REMNANT OF THE SPIRIT. A
ND WHAT DID THAT ONE DO WHILE
HE WAS SEEKING A GODLY OFFSPRING?
TAKE HEED THEN TO YOUR SPIRIT,
AND LET NO ONE DEAL TREACHEROUSLY
AGAINST THE WIFE OF YOUR YOUTH....
MALACHI 2:13-15 NASB

It's clear that God expects us to honour our marriage vows. God even states that He is a witness! Whether vows are spoken in church, in front a registrar or a judge, a higher witness is involved when people choose to enter the covenant of marriage.

- Ask God's forgiveness if you have broken your marriage vows in the past.

- Ask God to help you keep your vows.

Live a Life Without Loopholes

It's inevitable that when the Old Testament is examined someone will question its validity in the light of the New Testament. That's why it's important to CROSS-reference it as we have done before. Let's find out what Jesus has to say on the subject. In Matthew 19 Jesus clarifies some important things. Jesus was talking to the Pharisees; they were people who knew the law, lived by the law and were experts at finding loopholes. A little like the attitude we find in our society today the Pharisees were looking at reasons for divorce. They wanted clarification if they could divorce for every and any reason. They were really asking if covenant was still relevant to their culture. Jesus' answer is really interesting!

Jesus didn't ask them to look around them and decide what was right by what society was doing. He didn't say, "Hey, don't worry about it! I'm here; now you can do what you like. Instead, He pointed them to God's original plan. "He answered, "Have you not read that he who created them from the beginning made them male and female, and said, 'Therefore a man shall leave his father and his mother and hold fast to his wife, and the two shall become one flesh'? So they are no longer two but one flesh. What therefore God has joined, let not man separate." Matthew 19:4-6

Jesus reminds the Pharisees about the first

covenant. He skips most of the Old Testament because the model of that society wasn't part of God's original plan. After the fall marriage had become corrupted. Instead, He quotes the beginning of the book of Genesis. He reminds them that in a covenant God joins the husband and wife together, God views them as one so divorce shouldn't be in anyone's mentality. In fact, He reiterates that man (which, of course, included the Pharisees responsible for upholding the law) should not separate a husband and wife.

When the Pharisees push a bit further because of the traditions they kept regarding divorce, Jesus tells them bluntly that it's only like that because of the hardness of people's hearts. That was difficult for everyone to swallow, the disciples included! If it was difficult for them to stomach it shouldn't surprise us that our society has a problem with it too. Think about it! Both society and religion had a way of dealing with unhappy couples, and Jesus tells them it's not acceptable.

Sometimes having a CROSS-cultural marriage will go directly against everything that is normal in society. When He was challenged by what was common in society Jesus reminded them of the original plan and told them 'in the beginning, it was not so', in other words, that wasn't the way marriage was designed. Jesus challenges our behaviour in relationships; He also challenges our heart attitudes. When it comes down to it, a lot of marriage issues are matters of the heart. We often assume that things became a lot easier because of Christ's death on the cross but actually in some areas Jesus raised the bar.

Everyone (disciples included) baulked at the next thing that Jesus had to say, "And I say to you: whoever divorces his wife, except for sexual immorality, and marries another, commits adultery." Matthew 19:9 ESVUK. That was not music to their ears just as it is not something that people want to hear today. The disciples said to him, "If such is the case of a man with his wife, it is better not to marry. Matthew 19:10. We have to accept though that these are 'red-letter' words; they are the words of Christ. No 'progressive' society should have a voice in our lives which is louder than God's.

- Did you think that covenant meant this?

- How does it change your commitment to each other?

- Read 'Covenant or Contract' by Craig Hill to get a deeper understanding of covenant.

We're starting to get a really clear picture of what God means by covenant. If you want to have a CROSS-cultural marriage, then it's important to give it a good foundation. Just as you would never dream of building a home without having a firm base, you should give attention to your foundation in marriage to make sure it can stand.

A prenuptial agreement is probably the shakiest of

all foundations to build upon because it is preparing for fail-ure. By nature, it's declaring a lack of trust in the other's commitment. God's prenuptial agreement goes something like this, 'You are in this for life, it will work if you follow My plan, let me be involved in the building project, and you will have something beautiful. You can be sure I'll keep my word, now keep yours'. See the difference?

Now let's look back at Malachi chapter two be-cause there are some important keys to a healthy marriage found within these verses. In verses 13 and 14 we can see that:

- God takes vows seriously

- There are consequences for breaking those vows.

- He views marriage as a covenant

- He expects people to stay faithful

Verse 15 holds an incredible key which is often over-looked. It takes something which makes this seem too dif-ficult, to something that is very possible.

"BUT NOT ONE HAS DONE SO WHO HAS A REMNANT OF THE SPIRIT.
AND WHAT DID THAT ONE DO WHILE SEEKING A GODLY OFFSPRING?
TAKE HEED THEN TO YOUR SPIRIT, AND LET NO ONE DEAL TREACHEROUSLY
AGAINST THE WIFE OF YOUR YOUTH."
MALACHI 2:15 (AMP)

When someone is submitted to God and listening to the voice of the Holy Spirit; then many difficulties in marriage can be avoided. It's a huge indictment to say that anyone who doesn't honour their covenant doesn't have a remnant of God's Spirit. God uses it as a warning and gives it a double emphasis here, "Take heed then to your spirit"! God wants to be a voice in our lives helping us to keep our covenant. He not only is a witness to marriage but He takes an active role!

The secret to a CROSS-cultural marriage is living by the Spirit! Time and time again through Galatians chapter five we are urged to walk in the Spirit. That's the secret to all relationships, and it is even more important in marriage.

If we live by the Spirit, let us also walk by the Spirit. Let us not become conceited, provoking one another,
envying one another.
Galatians 5:25,26

Transformation isn't easy especially if you try to do it on your own. If you are doing something that is cultural, it is likely to be a deeply ingrained habit. It takes God's power (not your willpower or legalism) to break that habit and establish a new Godly pattern.

For when we died with Christ we were set free from the power of sin.
Romans 6:7 (NLT)

†-Referencing Headship & Submission

CROSS Referencing Headship & Submission

Earlier we looked at the extremes of belief in a very emotive area. 'Headship and Submission' has long been a volatile topic in the Church. A history of abuse and misuse of scriptures has caused this to be one of the most controversial issues in marriage.

The Battle Lines

Imagine a line which represents the beliefs people hold about headship and submission. With misogynistic men (the hatred of, contempt for, or prejudice against women or girls) being on one end of the line and women with feminazi beliefs (women seeking superiority over men) on the other. Those two polar opposite views are like bookends on that line with a broad range of ideas that fall somewhere in between.

MISOGYNY _____ FEMINAZI

God created both male and female. He created both in His image and He created both to have a relationship with Him. In Romans 2:11 we are told that God shows no partiality. In other words, he doesn't favour one sex more than the other. Galatians 3:28 backs this up. In fact, God's Word makes a strong stand against bias! We are all one in Christ.

> "THERE IS NEITHER JEW NOR GREEK,
> THERE IS NEITHER SLAVE NOR FREE,
> THERE IS **NO MALE AND FEMALE,**
> FOR YOU ARE ALL **ONE** IN CHRIST JESUS."
> GALATIANS 3:28 (ESV)

This verse takes an eraser and removes the battle lines. There should be no battle of the sexes! It eradicates sexism, racism, and slavery in a few simple words. If only we would live that way!

DIFFERENT BUT NOT WRONG

Men and women have both been created in God's image, but they are not the same. I know that's obvious, but sometimes it's worth spelling it out! In the book of Genesis, the story of Eve's creation from Adam's side unfolds. God removed a rib (a chamber or capacity) from Adam and formed Eve. In doing so, He created two unique humans. They are distinctive, with individual qualities and attributes and gifts.

Just as we can be culturally wired to believe someone of another cultural background is of less value or inherently wrong the same mistake can be made of men and women. Gender prejudice is alive and kicking as hard as ethnocentrism. Some cultures are hardwired to believe that one sex is lesser than the other, and it manifests in extreme ways. Abuse whether physical, spiritual or emotional should never be part of a marriage or any other relationship.

Watch out for the subliminal messages you send to each other! The following tweet illustrates the point quite well.

"MARRIAGE IS MOSTLY ABOUT KNOWING WHICH HAND TOWELS YOU CAN USE AND WHICH ONES ARE FOR THE BETTER PEOPLE WHO VISIT YOUR WIFE'S HOME."
TROY JOHNSON

Although it's funny, do you see the problem here? Another guy called Jost tweeted

"BEFORE I GOT MARRIED I DIDN'T EVEN KNOW THERE WAS A WRONG WAY TO PUT THE MILK BACK IN THE FRIDGE."

While the Bible won't teach you about hand towels or milk, it does give us very clear relationship guidelines. Take Galatians 5:26, for instance! "Let us not become conceited, provoking one another, envying one another."

- Can you identify areas in your relationship where sexism is present?

- What does it look like in your relationship?

- Do you have a deep set belief that you are better than your spouse?

- Ask God for help to eradicate prejudice from your relationship.

- Ask forgiveness if you have been guilty of putting each other down.

When Different Became Harder.

So why did it all get more difficult? If God designed both sexes in His image and created marriage why is it so hard? There are many consequences of the fall. It seems that almost everything became more difficult after that event. Work became harder than before; fulfilling responsibilities became more of a burden and to cap it all relationships were also impacted. The tension and conflict between the sexes arose as a result of the fall.

Genesis 3:16
To the woman he said, "I will make your pains in childbearing very severe; with painful labour you will give birth to children. Your desire will be for your husband, and he will rule over you."

After the fall the roles and responsibilities of both Adam and Eve became much more challenging. While Eve had to bear the pain of childbirth, Adam had to sweat to accomplish his work. They both could expect pain in their work but in addition, they could expect pain in their relationship.

This section of Genesis 3:16 is often misunderstood. "Your desire will be for your husband, and he will rule over you." To truly understand this scripture it needs to be cross-referenced with Genesis 4:7 NASB "If you do well, will not your countenance be lifted up? And if you do not do well, sin is crouching at the door; and its desire is for you, but you must master it." God's warning to Cain is that there is going to be a battle for supremacy. The verse mirrors what we see in Genesis 3:16 and gives us a better understanding of what the curse is.

The curse isn't that women will desire their husbands in a loving way, the curse is that women will want supremacy over their husbands. Equally the part in Genesis 3:16 which says "he will rule over you." Is not a command for men to follow. The type of ruling here is clearly part of the curse. It's the effect of sin; sin makes men treat women harshly. Sin causes men to rule over their wives in a dictatorship fashion.

The power struggle commenced in the garden as a result of the curse. This is the reason why men tend to substitute the word headship for 'dominance' and women translate 'submission' as 'be a doormat'.

When we CROSS-reference these roles it becomes very clear how we should treat each other. Ephesians 5 has been subject to much misteaching, but when we read it in light of this revelation, it takes on a different meaning. Instead of starting to read at verse 22 we need to go back to verse 21. Which asks us to, "Submit to one another out of reverence for Christ". Our motivation must no longer be selfish; our inducement needs to be because of Christ.

God knows the tendencies we are fighting against, and that is why he instructs women to submit to their husbands in verse 22. He knows about the curse! Husbands in verse 25 he explains how you can fight against your propensity to be harsh. Verse 33 instructs a husband to love his wife as much as he loves himself. So, when you read the verses in context, it all starts falling into place and making sense.

The following verse in Philippians is worth memorising. It is important that we receive God's transforming power to break the old ways of doing things. If both of you put this into practice, your marriage will be much closer to a CROSS-cultural one.

DO NOTHING FROM SELFISHNESS OR EMPTY CONCEIT
[THROUGH FACTIONAL MOTIVES, OR STRIFE],
BUT WITH [AN ATTITUDE OF] HUMILITY
[BEING NEITHER ARROGANT NOR SELF-RIGHTEOUS],

REGARD OTHERS AS MORE IMPORTANT THAN YOURSELVES.
PHILIPPIANS 2:3 (AMP)

This verse suggests an antidote for the curse. It helps us to get back to Genesis when husband and wife worked together in harmony. It takes a couple from being worlds apart to living a fulfilling life together.

- Has this side of your relationship fallen into the curse or blessing category?

- Can you identify personal tendencies to desire to rule over each other?

- Ask forgiveness from each other for the times you have fallen into the trap of wrestling with each other for supremacy.

We hope that in reading this book, you have learned something new about yourself, your spouse and your relationship. We trust that in the learning process you haven't just acquired knowledge and understanding but that you have gained wisdom. Wisdom which will help you both blend together. Bringing Worlds Together is the first in a series of books designed to help you in that journey. Other books in the series include Adjusting Expectations, Family Connections and Improving Communication.

FOR MORE INFORMATION ON THIS AND OTHER ROLES YOU CAN READ OUR OTHER BOOK ON THE SUBJECT
'HIS PART, HER PART & GOD'S PART'.

BIBLIOGRAPHY

Chapman, Dr. Gary 'The 5 Love Languages'
Chicago, Northfield Pub.1995.

Fraser-Smith, Janet. Love Across Latitudes 6th Edition. A Workbook on
Cross-Cultural Marriage. Gilead Books Publishing. 2015

Kircher Jake & Melissa. Does Media Distort Love? A look at our cor-
rupting views of romance, relationships and sexuality. Relevant Maga-
zine. April 12, 2011
http://www.relevantmagazine.com/life/relationship/features/25275-
distorting-love#D1zDB4xq0I7yLGKY.99

Lewis, Richard D. When Cultures Collide, 3rd Edition: Leading Across
Cultures Finland, WS Bookwell 2006

Lubin, Gus. These Diagrams Reveal How To Negotiate With People
Around The World. Mar. 25, 2014. Business Insider
http://www.businessinsider.com/communication-charts-around-the-
world-2014-3

Migdon Stuart: Jesus Take the Wheel: 7 Keys to a Transformed Life with
God. Western Australia. Wine Press Publishing. 2008

Parker-Pope Tara, Love on the Global Brain, The New York Times May,
24. 2010.
http://well.blogs.nytimes.com/2010/05/24/love-on-the-global-brain/

Smith-Cannoy, Heather. Insincere Commitments: Human Rights Trea-
ties, Abusive States, and Citizen Activism Georgetown University Press,
2012

Piper, John. Racial Harmony and Interracial Marriage
desiringGod.org January. 16, 2005
http://www.desiringgod.org/messages/racial-harmony-and-interra-
cial-marriage

BIOGRAPHY

Roy and Lainey Hitchman met at university in the late 80's. Roy was studying aeronautical engineering and was on the university rowing team. Lainey was studying English and had a love of coffee. They got married during their student years, and God started to stir their hearts to help people navigate their relationships.

They have been ministering to families since 1993. Their passion for working with relationships led to them founding a ministry called 'Hitched' which encompasses working with a wide variety of relationships through a number of stages in life. Roy and Lainey share hard-hitting yet life-giving principles through transparency and humour.

Roy and Lainey spend much of their time speaking, writing and reaching out to those who need some encouragement in the area of relationships. When they aren't travelling, they enjoy spending time with their family, Ryan, Beth, Erin and their son-in-law Jonathan although it takes a little organisation to get everyone in one place at one time.

If you would like to learn more about their ministry, find more resources or get in touch you can contact them through www.hitched-together.com or www.lifeforsingles.com. If you would like them to speak at your church, seminar or conference, then please contact them via email at info@hitchedtogether.com

Printed in Poland
by Amazon Fulfillment
Poland Sp. z o.o., Wrocław